Let's Go to a Car Race

By Cate Foley

Welcome
Books

Children's Press
A Division of Scholastic Inc.
New York / Toronto / London / Auckland / Sydney
Mexico City / New Delhi / Hong Kong
Danbury, Connecticut

Photo Credits: Cover, pp. 5, 7, 9, 21 by Maura Boruchow; pp. 11, 13, 15, 17, 19, 21 © Corbis
Contributing Editor: Jennifer Silate
Book Design: Victoria Johnson

Library of Congress Cataloging-in-Publication Data

Foley, Cate.
  Let's go to a car race / by Cate Foley.
    p. cm. -- (Weekend fun)
  Includes bibliographical references and index.
  ISBN 0-516-23191-x (lib. bdg.) -- ISBN 0-516-29581-0 (pbk.)
  1. Automobile racing--Juvenile literature. [1. Automobile racing.] I. Title. II. Series.

GV1029 .F59 2001
796.72--dc21

                                              2001017273

Contents

We are going to a car race today.

4

5

My dad pays for us to get in.

6

We sit in the **grandstand**.

8

The **drivers** are getting ready to race.

They put on their **helmets**.

The race starts when the green flag drops.

The cars go fast around the **racetrack**.

They will go around many times.

15

A man waves a white flag.

This means that there is one **lap** left to race.

17

A car crosses the finish line.

It is the winner!

18

We had fun at the car race.

New Words

drivers (**dry**-vuhrz) people who operate vehicles

grandstand (**grand**-stand) the main place where people sit when they watch a sports event

helmets (**hehl**-mihts) coverings to protect the head

lap (**lap**) one time around something

racetrack (**rays**-trak) a course on which races are run

To Find Out More

Books
Famous Finishes
by Ann G. Gaines
Chelsea House Publishers

Race Car
by Caroline Bingham and Deni Bown
DK Publishing

Web Site
Rockets on Wheels: Electronic Field Trip
http://www.pbs.org/tal/racecars
Build your own race car and learn about racing on this Web site.

Index

About the Author
Cate Foley writes and edits books for children. She lives in New Jersey with her husband and son.

Reading Consultants
Kris Flynn, Coordinator, Small School District Literacy, The San Diego County Office of Education

Shelly Forys, Certified Reading Recovery Specialist, W.J. Zahnow Elementary School, Waterloo, IL

Sue McAdams, Fomer President of the North Texas Reading Council of the IRA, and Early Literary Consultant, Dallas, TX

24